Good Night, Willie Lee,
I'll See You in the Morning

Alice Walker

Published in Great Britain by The Women's Press Ltd, 1987
A member of the Namara Group
34 Great Sutton Street, London EC1V 0DX

Reprinted 1995

First published in the United States of America by Dial Press, 1979, reprinted by
Harcourt Brace Jovanovich, 1984

Acknowledgements:
'Early Losses: a Requiem' appeared in New Letters, Vol. 41-2 (Winter, 1974).
Copyright © 1974 by the Curators of the University of Missouri. 'Light baggage'
and 'On Stripping Bark from Myself' appeared in The American Poetry Review, Vol. 6,
No. 1, 1977. 'Talking to my grandmother who died poor' and 'Good Night, Willie
Lee, I'll See You in the Morning' appeared in The Iowa Review, Vol. 6, No. 2, 1975.
'Janie Crawford' appeared in Aphrs, Vol. 5, No. 3, 1964. 'Facing the Way', 'The
Abduction of Saints', and 'Forgiveness' appeared in Freedomways, Vol. 15, No. 4,
1975. 'Your Soul Shines' and 'The Instant of Our Parting' appeared in Nimrod, Vol.
21, No. 2/Vol. 22, No. 1, 1977.

British Library Cataloguing-in-Publication Data
Walker, Alice, 1944–
    Goodnight, Willie Lee, I'll see you in the morning
    I. Title
    811'.54   PS3573.A425

ISBN 0 7043 4063 1

Printed and bound in Great Britain by BPC Paperbacks Ltd, Aylesbury, Bucks

Dedication

Many years ago, a young romantic girl who had always modestly refrained from admitting her most secret belief (that her own people possessed the lion's share of beauty and goodness in the world) perceived the end was coming for them as they were and set out for the Last Land. There she wished to collect the saltysweet drops of sweat—the price of her people's goodness and beauty—from their rapidly freezing faces.

Wishing at least to observe what could not be prevented, she expected to see the end of sweaty beauty, and she did.

Everywhere she went she found that earlier visitors not so reverent as she (for with bullets and hatred they had come) had iced flat the warm, round faces she would have loved. Perhaps, here and there, a face had escaped and it would hold her rapt. She would quickly press it inside a large notebook she carried and her tears were payment for the theft.

But these were the faces of the old, those who would soon be dead.

She became quite discouraged.

But then she began to hear about a man no one could describe without first saying: "Well, he was a quiet man . . . ." and her flagging heart revived and she began to look for him.

In the fields, underneath the trees, in small country stores, in the shabby new schools that housed the people's children.

Under the very noses of those who iced people daily, she looked.

But she did not find him.

The people said, "The quiet man always said, 'Let the people decide.'" And, though it did not seem quite the revolutionary thing to some of them, if the people wanted—in a particular village—to operate sewing machines, he would sit and sew with them. If they wanted to cook ribs, he would wash the pots. If they wanted to march, he was on the line.

If someone asked him anything (because they thought he was wise even though he had been to the white man's best schools) he would only reply, "Let the people decide."

"Oh, he was a quiet man," they told the romantic young girl, "and he loved women not just to lie with but he would stand up with them when no one else would. A quiet young man. A woman could speak in his company. A man could touch his shoulder with his hand and call out his own heart for review."

It so happened that the romantic young girl's own heart hungered for just this last experience.

But she never found him.

Even before she began her search he had disappeared from that land. He changed his name, they said; took his mother's name. Returned to his mother's far country, which was Africa.

The young romantic girl never saw his face, never heard his voice, never felt him stand up beside her, though it reassured her that he must be somewhere.

He became a memory of someone she had never known, a high standard.

And perhaps no one had known him. Perhaps he did not exist. Perhaps the people made up the quiet man because they needed him to exist. Perhaps if he did exist he was a fraud. So many people are.

But she chooses not to believe anything except that he does exist, and she dedicates this book to him, wherever in the world he is.

. . . and to my five fine brothers: Fred, William, James, Robert, and Curtis

(and my friend Gloria)

. . . and in memory of our father's shining eyes.

Confession

Did This Happen to Your Mother?
Did Your Sister Throw Up a Lot?

I love a man who is not worth
my love.
Did this happen to your mother?
Did your grandmother wake up
for no good reason
in the middle of the night?

I thought love could be controlled.
It cannot.
Only behavior can be controlled.
By biting your tongue purple
rather than speak.
Mauling your lips.
Obliterating his number
too thoroughly
to be able to phone.

Love has made me sick.

Did your sister throw up a lot?
Did your cousin complain
of a painful knot
in her back?
Did your aunt always
seem to have something else
troubling her mind?

I thought love would adapt itself
to my needs.
But needs grow too fast;
they come up like weeds.
Through cracks in the conversation.

Through silences in the dark.
Through everything you thought was concrete.

Such needful love has to be chopped out
or forced to wilt back,
poisoned by disapproval
from its own soil.

This is bad news, for the conservationist.

My hand shakes before this killing.
My stomach sits jumpy in my chest.
My chest is the Grand Canyon
sprawled empty
over the world.

Whoever he is, he is not worth all this.

And I will never
unclench my teeth long enough
to tell him so.

More Love to His Life

Though I, at the time, had no one
and furthermore was dutifully told
how much he loved his wife,
he feared, he said,
I would reject him.
And so, the burden of adding more love
to his life
fell on me.

How could I refuse?
He needed the love of everyone.
I needed to understand this
though it did violence,
as they say,
to my heart.
Having no rights. No claims
to make, I could not even coherently
protest.

My heart, however, sent out darts
and messages
like red flags:
You are sending me away!
Stop! You are hurting me!
I love you more than anything
in my life!

But I laughed, over the phone,
as it occurred to me
that perhaps *he* was comic
instead of myself.

Gift

He said: Here is my soul.
I did not want his soul
but I am a Southerner
and very polite.
I took it lightly
as it was offered. But did not
chain it down.
I loved it and tended
it. I would hand it back
as good as new.

He said: How dare you want
my soul! Give it back!
How greedy you are!
It is a trait
I had not noticed
before!

I said: But your soul
never left you. It was only
a heavy thought from
your childhood
passed to me for safekeeping.

But he never believed me.
Until the end
he called me possessive
and held his soul
so tightly
it shrank
to fit his hand

Never Offer Your Heart
to Someone Who Eats Hearts

Never offer your heart
to someone who eats hearts
who finds heartmeat
delicious
but not rare
who sucks the juices
drop by drop
and bloody-chinned
grins
like a God.

Never offer your heart
to a heart gravy lover.
Your stewed, overseasoned
heart consumed
he will sop up your grief
with bread
and send it shuttling
from side to side
in his mouth
like bubblegum.

If you find yourself
in love
with a person
who eats hearts
these things
you must do:

Freeze your heart
immediately.
Let him—next time

he examines your chest—
find your heart cold
flinty and unappetizing.

Refrain from kissing
lest he in revenge
dampen the spark
in your soul.

Now,
sail away to Africa
where holy women
await you
on the shore—
long having practiced the art
of replacing hearts
with God
and Song.

Threatened

Threatened by my rising need
he writes
he is afraid
he may fail me
in performance.
But—I tell him—
I have failed
all my life—
only with you
do I nearly succeed.
My heart—which I feel
freezing a bit each day
to this man—nonetheless
cries: Don't leave her!
Don't go! She is counting
on you!
When we talk about it
nothing to still my fear
of his fear
is said

it is this fear
that now devours
desire.

My Husband Says

My husband says
this shortness of breath
and feeling of falling down a well
I suffer
in the half-life I share
with my lover
will soon cease to plague me.
That love, like war,
escalates
each side raising its demands
for what it wants
as emotions rise
higher and higher
and what was unthought of in the beginning
becomes the inevitable result.

"Soon you will write
you can not live without him
no matter that he has a wife.
He will tell you
the 1,000 miles separating you
is crushing to his soul.
As for me,
I love no one now
except you.
But if I am ever asked
in your presence
if this is true,
please don't take offense
at the vehemence
of my negative
reply."

Confession

All winter long
I've borne the knife that presses
without ceasing
against my heart.
Despising lies
I have told everyone
the truth:
Truth is killing me.

The Instant of Our Parting

I said: I cannot tell you
how much I do not believe
in you
the instant we part.

I said: I lived in limbo
that whole summer
wondering if your love for me
would survive your flight
home.

I said: I am better now
that the instant we part
the instant of our parting
is with me always.

He Said:

He said: I want you to be happy.
He said: I love you so.
Then he was gone.
For two days I was happy.
For two days, he loved me so.
After that, I was on my own.

The Last Time

The last time
I was afflicted by love
I murdered the man.
But that was in an earlier century
another country
a hotter climate
and death proved him
a foreign transient
like any other.

After the Shrink

Without my melancholia I am lonely
dazed. Under the doctor's care
I can remember nothing very long
that is sad.
Round and round I travel
enduring my comfort.

At First

At first I did not fight it.
I *loved* the suffering.
It was being alive!
I felt my heart pump the blood
that splashed my insides
with red flowers;
I savored my grief
like chilled wine.

I did not know my life
was being shredded
by an expert.

It was my friend Gloria
who saved me. Whose glance said "Really,
you've got to be kidding. Other
women have already done this
sort of suffering for you,
or so I thought."

On Stripping Bark from Myself…

Janie Crawford

i love the way Janie Crawford

left her husbands   the one who wanted
to change her into a mule
and the other who tried to interest her
in being a queen
a woman unless she submits is neither a mule
nor a queen
though like a mule she may suffer
and like a queen pace
the floor

Moody

I am a moody woman
my temper as black as my brows
as sharp as my nails
as impartial as a flood
that is seeking, seeking, seeking
always
somewhere to stop.

Now That the Book Is Finished

Now that the book is finished,
now that I know my characters
will live,
I can love my child again.
She need sit no longer
at the back of my mind,
the lonely sucking of her thumb
a giant stopper in my throat.

Having Eaten Two Pillows

(for Bessie Head)*

Having eaten two pillows
in the middle of the night
having stumbled from bullets
my close friends have fired
having loved all those fully
that I love
and still not loving
all those to whom time
has not brought grace
ambition raises itself:
to survive my life
"just anyone"
        hello
though I know quite well
the words to say goodbye.

*In some of the fiction of South African writer Bessie
Head, the ambition of her characters is not to be extraordi-
nary or considered extraordinary but to become "just any-
one," which is perceived as the correct relationship to other
people and to the world.

I feel this is also a correct alternative to despair, or, in
some cases, suicide.

Light baggage

(for Zora, Nella, Jean)*

there is a magic
lingering after people
to whom success is merely personal.
who, when the public prepares a feast
for their belated acceptance parties,
pack it up like light baggage
and disappear into the swamps of Florida
or go looking for newer Gods
in the Oak tree country
of Pennsylvania.
Or decide, quite suddenly, to try nursing,
midwifery, anonymous among the sick and the poor.
Stories about such people
tell us little;
and if a hundred photographs survive
each one will show a different face.
someone out of step. alone out there, absorbed;
fishing in the waters of experience
a slouched back against the shoulders
of the world.

*Zora Neale Hurston, Nella Larson, and Jean Toomer
wrote and published their best work during the twenties and
thirties. At some point in their careers each of them left the
"career" of writing and went off seeking writing's very
heart: life itself. Zora went back to her native Florida where
she lived in a one-room cabin and raised her own food; Jean
Toomer became a Quaker and country philosopher in Bucks
County, Pennsylvania; and Nella Larson, less well known
than either Hurston or Toomer, became a nurse.

On Stripping Bark from Myself

(for Jane, who said trees die from it)

because women are expected to keep silent about
their close escapes I will not keep silent
and if I am destroyed (naked tree!) someone will
    please
mark the spot
where I fall and know I could not live
silent in my own lies
hearing their "how *nice* she is!"
whose adoration of the retouched image
I so despise.

No. I am finished with living
for what my mother believes
for what my brother and father defend
for what my lover elevates
for what my sister, blushing, denies or rushes
to embrace.

I find my own
small person
a standing self
against the world
an equality of wills
I finally understand.

Besides:

My struggle was always against
an inner darkness: I carry within myself
the only known keys
to my death—to unlock life, or close it shut

forever. A woman who loves wood grains, the color
  yellow
and the sun, I am happy to fight
all outside murderers
as I see I must.

Early Losses: a Requiem

Early Losses: a Requiem

PART I

Nyanu was appointed
as my Lord. The husband chosen
by the elders
before my birth.
He sipped wine with
my father
and when I was born
brought a parrot as
his gift
to play with me.
Paid baskets of grain
and sweet berries
to make me fat
for his pleasure.

Omunu was my playmate
who helped consume
Nyanu's gifts.
Our fat selves grew
together
knee and knee.
It was Omunu I wished
to share my tiny
playing house.

Him I loved as the sun
must seek and chase
its own reflection
across the sky.

My brothers, before you
turn away—

The day the savages came
to ambush our village
it was Nyanu who struggled
bravely
Omunu ran and hid
behind his parents' house.
He was a coward but
only nine
as was I; who trembled
beside him as we two
were stolen away
Nyanu's dead body
begging remembrance
of his tiny morsel
taken from his mouth.
Nor was I joyful that he was dead
only glad that now I would not have
to marry him.

Omunu clasped my hands
within the barkcloth pouch
and I his head
a battered flower
bent low
upon its stalk
Our cries pounded back
into our throats
by thudding blows
we could not see
our mothers' cries
at such a distance
we could not hear
and over the miles
we feasted on homesickness
our mothers' tears and
the dew
all we consumed of homeland
before we left.

At the great water Omunu fought
to stay with me
at such a tender age
our hearts we set
upon each other
as the retreating wave
brings its closest friend
upon its back.
We cried out in words
that met an echo
and Omunu vanished
down a hole that
smelled of blood and
excrement and death
and I was "saved"
for sport among
the sailors of the crew.
Only nine, upon a ship. My mouth
my body a mystery
that opened with each tearing
lunge. Crying for Omunu
who was not seen
again
by these eyes.

Listen to your sister, singing
in the field.
My body forced to receive
grain and wild berries
and milk so I could seem
a likely wench
—my mother's child
sold for a price. My father's
child again for sale.
I prayed to all our Gods
"Come down to me"
Hoist the burden no child
was meant to bear
and decipher the prayer
from within each song
—the song despised—

my belly become a stronghold
for a stranger
who will not recall
when he is two
the contours of
his mother's face.
See the savages turn back
my lips
and with hot irons
brand me neck and thigh.

I could not see the horizon
for the sky
a burning eye
the sun, beloved in the shade,
became an enemy
a pestle pounding long
upon my head.
You walked with me.
And when day sagged into night
some one of you of my own
choice
shared my rest. Omunu
risen from the ocean
out of the stomachs of whales
the teeth of sharks
lying beside me sleeping
knee and knee.
We could not speak always
of hearts
for in the morning if they
sold you
how could I flatten
a wrinkled face?
The stupor of dread
made smooth the look
that to my tormentors
was born erased.
I mourned for you. And if you died
took out my heart upon my lap
and rested it.

29

See me old at thirty
my sack of cotton weighted
to the ground. My hair
enough to cover a marble
my teeth like rattles
made of chalk
my breath a whisper
of decay.
The slack of my belly
falling to my knees.
I shrink to become a tiny size
a delicate morsel
upon my mother's knee
prepared like bread. The shimmering
of the sun a noise
upon my head.

To the child that's left
I offer a sound
without a promise
a clue
of what it means.

The sound itself is all.

PART II
The Child

A sound like a small wind
finding the door of a
hollow reed
my mother's farewell
glocked up from the back
of her throat

the sound itself is all

all I have
to remember a mother
I scarcely knew.

"Omunu" to me; who never knew
what "Omunu" meant. Whether home
or man or trusted God. "Omunu."
Her only treasure,
and never spent.

In Uganda an Early King

In Uganda an early king chose
his wives
from among the straight and lithe
who natural as birds of paradise
and the wild poinsettias
grow

(Did you ever see Uganda women? Dainty
are their fingers
genteel their footsteps on the sand)
and he brought them behind
the palace to a place constructed
like a farmer's fattening pen
with slats raised off the ground
and nothing for
an escapable door
he force-fed them bran and milk
until the milk ran down their
chins
off the bulging mounds that filled
their skins

their eyes quite disappeared
they grew too fat to stand
but slithered to the hole
that poured their dinner
enormous seals

Because? *He liked fat wives*
they showed him prosperous!
and if they up and burst

or tore their straining skins
across the splintered floor,
why, like balloons,
he bought some more.

Forgive Me If My Praises

I

Forgive me if my praises
do not come easily
I do not praise myself
I am the cause of (he says)
my father's failure.
Protecting me
turned him into
a coward.
I, who curbed his temper
and shaped his life.
Me, who now can not praise
my work.

II

They said:
My father was not
a great man.
My father was a peasant
a serf.
The grandson of a slave.
My father was not a man.
They said.

III

Even so—
Let me surprise you

with my love
turned to fear
that I would gladly
pretend away

    IV

Open your arms.
Take me on your lap.
Sing me a blues.
Be B.B. King to my
Mean Woman.

    V

What I need I know
is a good satisfying love
with even one such as you
with open seed-sowing hands
on long arms
embracing me
with lips purple as
Tea Cake's

kisses warm

a shoulder firm
as the smooth
strong flanks of trees
to fight with me against
my evil dreams.

The Abduction of Saints

As it was with Christ, so it is with Malcolm
and with King.
Who could withstand the seldom flashing smile,
the call to dance among the swords and barbs
that were their words? The men leaning from
out the robes of saints,
good and wholly kind? Though come
at last to both fists clenched and Voice
to flatten the ears
of all the world.

You mock them who divide and keep score of what
each man gave. They gave us rebellion as pure love:
a beginning of the new man.

Christ too was man rebelling. Walking dusty roads,
        sweating
under the armpits. Loving the cool of evening beside
the ocean,
the people's greetings and barbecued chicken; cursing
        under
his breath
the bruise from his sandal and his donkey's diarrhea.
Don't let them fool you. He was himself a beginning
of the new man. His love in front.
His love and his necessary fist, behind. (Life,
ended at a point, always falls backward into the
little that was known of it.)

But see how this saint too is hung defenselessly
on walls, his strong hands pinned:
his pious look causes us to blush, for him.

He belongs to Caesar.

It is because his people stopped to tally and to count:
Perhaps he loved young men too much? Did he wear
    his hair
a bit too long, or short? Weren't the strategies
he proposed all wrong,
since of course they did not work?

It is because his people argued over him. Denounced
each other
in his name. When next they looked they hardly no-
    ticed
he no longer looked himself.

Who could imagine that timid form with Voice like
thunder
to make threats, a fist enlarged from decking mer-
    chants?
That milkwhite cheek, the bluebell eye, the cracked
heart of plaster
designed
for speedy decay.

Aha! said a cricket in the grass (ancient observer of
distracted cross examiners);

Now you've seen it, now you don't!

And the body
was stolen away.

Malcolm

Those who say they knew you
offer as proof
an image stunted
by perfection.
Alert for signs of the man
to claim, one must believe
they did not know you at all
nor can remember the small, less popular
ironies of the Saint:
that you learned to prefer
all women free
and enjoyed a joke
and loved to laugh.

Facing the Way

(in answer to your silly question)

(for algernon)

people have eaten fried fish
with the people
sewn on sewing machines
with the people
assaulted school and church
with the people
fought feet to feet
beside the people
have given their lives
to the people
but they have forgotten to shout
"i *adore* the people!"

so the people's tribunal approaches.

Streaking (a phenomenon following the sixties)

the students
went out
of their way
to say
they were not
hurting anyone
or damaging
property
as they streaked across the country—
vulnerable
as a rape victim's
character
after ten years
of public
executions
naked
as the decade
they were formed.

" 'Women of Color' Have Rarely Had The Opportunity to Write About Their Love Affairs"

(a found poem: The New York Review of Books, Nov. 30, 1972)

Since he had few intimate friends, and little
is known
about his private life,
it is of interest that Shirley Graham,
his second wife,
has now published an account
of their life together
in *His Truth Is Marching On*.

Unfortunately, however, her version of Du Bois's
career
is perhaps more revealing of herself
than of her late husband.
The gaps in Mrs. Du Bois's memoir
are more instructive
than her recollections.

She has nothing to say
about the internal drama
of the NAACP's birth.
She mentions Du Bois's conflict with
Washington
only in passing
and his debates with
Garvey
            not at all.
Instead she clutters her narrative
with lengthy accounts
of her father's
work
in the NAACP,
the food

Du Bois liked,
and the international celebrities
she was able to meet

                              because she was married
to Du Bois.

"Women of Color" have rarely had
the opportunity to write about their love
affairs.
There are no black legends comparable to
that of Heloise
and Abelard
or even of Bonnie
and Clyde.

Mrs. Du Bois (who was known as a writer
before she married)
seems to have wanted to fill this gap.

Her recollections, unfortunately, are a cloying
intrusion
into any serious effort
to understand
Du Bois.

She assumes her romance
with Du Bois
to be as interesting as any other aspect
of his career.

facing the way

the fundamental question about revolution
as lorraine hansberry was not afraid to know
is not simply whether i am willing to give up my life
but if i am prepared to give up my comfort:
clean sheets on my bed
the speed of the dishwasher
and my gas stove
gadgetless
but still preferable to cooking out of doors
over a fire of smouldering roots
my eyes raking the skies for planes
the hills for army tanks.
paintings i have revered stick against my walls
as unconcerned as saints
their perfection alone sufficient for their defense.
yet not one lifeline thrown by the artist
beyond the frame
reaches the boy whose eyes were target
for a soldier's careless aim
or the small girl whose body napalm
a hot bath after mass rape
transformed
or the old women who starve on muscatel
nightly
on the streets of New York.

it is shameful how hard it is for me to give
them up!
to cease this cowardly addiction
to art that transcends time
beauty that nourishes a ravenous spirit
but drags on the mind whose sale would patch

a roof
heat the cold rooms of children. replace an eye.
feed a life.

it does not comfort me now to hear
thepoorweshallhavewithusalways
(Christ should never have said this:
it makes it harder than ever to change)
just as it failed to comfort me
when i was poor.

talking to my grandmother
who died poor
(while hearing Richard Nixon declare
"I am not a crook.")

no doubt i will end my life as poor as you
without the wide veranda of your dream
on which to sit and fan myself slowly
without the tall drinks to cool my bored
unthirsty throat.
you will think: Oh, my granddaughter failed
to make something of herself
in the White Man's World!

but i really am not a crook
i am not descended from crooks
my father was not president of anything
and only secretary to the masons
where his dues were a quarter a week
which he did not shirk to pay.

that buys me a new dream
though i may stray
and lust after jewelry
and a small house by the sea:
yet i could give up even lust
in proper times
and open my doors to strangers
or live in one room.
that is the new dream.

in the meantime i hang on
fighting addiction
to the old dream
knowing i must train myself to want
not one bit more
than what i need to keep me alive

working
and recognizing beauty
in your
        so nearly
undefeated face.

January 10, 1973

i sit for hours staring at my own right hand
wondering if it would help me shoot the judge
who called us chimpanzees from behind his bench
and would it help pour sweet arsenic
into the governor's coffeepot
or drop cyanide into yours.
you don't have to tell me;
i understand these are the clichéd fantasies
of twenty-five million longings
that spring spontaneously to life
every generation.
it is hard for me to write
what everybody already knows;
still, it appears to me
i have pardoned the dead
enough.

Forgiveness

Your Soul Shines

Your soul shines
like the sides of a fish.
My tears are salty
my grief is deep.
Come live in me again.
Each day I walk along the edges
of the tall rocks.

forgiveness

each time I order her to go
for a ruler and face her small
grubby outstretched palm
i feel before hitting it
the sting in my own
and become my mother
preparing to chastise me
on a gloomy Saturday afternoon
long ago. and glaring down into my own sad
and grieving face i forgive myself
for whatever crime i may
have done. as i wish i could always
forgive myself
then as now.

Even as I hold you

Even as I hold you
I think of you as someone gone
far, far away. Your eyes the color
of pennies in a bowl of dark honey
bringing sweet light to someone else
your black hair slipping through my fingers
is the flash of your head going
around a corner
your smile, breaking before me,
the flippant last turn
of a revolving door,
emptying you out, changed,
away from me.

Even as I hold you
I am letting go.

"Good Night, Willie Lee,
I'll See You in the Morning"

Looking down into my father's
dead face
for the last time
my mother said without
tears, without smiles
without regrets
but with *civility*
"Good night, Willie Lee, I'll see you
in the morning."
And it was then I knew that the healing
of all our wounds
is forgiveness
that permits a promise
of our return
at the end.

Also of interest:

Alice Walker
Her Blue Body Everything We Know
Earthling Poems 1965–1990 Complete

Pulitzer prize-winning author Alice Walker has been writing
poetry since the summer of 1965. This is the first complete
collection of her work, containing many previously unpublished
poems, plus new introductions to those previously collected.
Bringing valuable new insights and reflections, this beautiful,
definitive volume offers a unique look at a remarkable writer's
development and provides a fascinating retrospective on the
political, social and spiritual issues of the last three decades.

'One cannot read Walker and remain unmoved.' *Books and
Bookmen*

**'One of the most important, grieving, graceful and
honest writers ever to come into print.'** June Jordan

Poetry £9.99/ £15.95
ISBN 0 7043 4322 3   Paperback/ISBN 0 7043 5061 0   Hardback

Alice Walker
The Complete Stories

Now in one superb and definitive gift volume come the complete
stories of Alice Walker. Gleaned from her experiences as a child
and young adult in the Deep South, and from her life as an
activist, lover, mother, teacher, wife and friend, this resonant
collection showcases three decades of work from one of the
most gifted writers of our time.

**'Alice Walker conveys the passion, serenity and sense of
freedom that comes from her ability to defy traditions.'**
Essence

**'Alice Walker admirers will yearn to have these on their
shelves.'** *Guardian*

Fiction £15.99
ISBN 0 7043 5066 1

Alice Walker
The Color Purple

Set in the harsh, segregated world of the Deep South, Alice
Walker's compelling and prize-winning novel tells the story of
Celie. Raped by the man she calls father, her two children taken
away from her, and forced into an ugly, loveless marriage, Celie
has no one to talk to but God. Then she meets Shug Avery, singer
and magic woman – and discovers, not the pain of female rivalry,
but the love and support of women.

A massive international bestseller, and winner of the Pulitzer Prize
for Fiction in 1983, *The Color Purple* is also an internationally
successful film, produced by Steven Spielberg.

'Walker's voice has power, poise and conviction.' *Times
Literary Supplement*

'She is one of the most gifted writers of her country.'
Isabel Allende

Fiction £5.99
ISBN 0 7043 3905 6